The Glucose Goddess Method Cookbook Inspired By Jessie Inchauspe's Teachings

Quick and Easy Recipes For Maintaining and Balancing Healthy Blood Sugar Levels

Michelle C. Huff

Copyright © [2024] by Michelle C. Huff. All rights reserved.

No part of this publication may be reproduced, distributed, or transmitted in any form or by any means, including photocopying, recording, or other electronic or mechanical methods, without the prior written permission of the author, except in the case of brief quotations embodied in critical reviews and certain other non-commercial uses permitted by copyright law.

Disclaimer

This book, The Glucose Goddess Method Cookbook Inspired By Jessie Inchauspe's Teachings, is an independent publication authored by Michelle C. Huff. While inspired by Jessie Inchauspe's teachings, it is not written by Jessie Inchauspe nor directly affiliated with her. All content, including recipes and advice, is based on the author's interpretation and research.

The content provided in this book is for informational and educational purposes only. It is not intended to be a substitute for professional medical advice, diagnosis, or treatment. Always seek the advice of your physician or other qualified health providers with any questions you may have regarding a medical condition. The author and publisher assume no responsibility for any adverse effects that may result from the use or application of the recipes or guidance contained within this book.

The reader assumes full responsibility for consulting a qualified health professional before starting any new dietary or health program. The author and publisher are not liable for any personal or professional outcomes associated with the application of the material in this book.

Introduction

The concept for The Glucose Goddess Method Cookbook was born out of an understanding of a common challenge faced by many people: the daily struggle with fatigue, strong cravings, and finding the right balance for sustained energy levels. This state of being isn't just an inconvenience—it affects every aspect of life, from productivity and focus to overall well-being. Inspired by Jessie Inchauspe's research and insights on blood sugar management, this cookbook was crafted to serve as a bridge between understanding the science behind glucose regulation and applying it in a way that makes sense in the kitchen.

Jessie Inchauspe's book, Glucose Revolution, opened the door to the realization that managing blood sugar is not only essential for people with specific health conditions but for everyone who wants to live with more vitality. The lessons from her work showed that the key to sustainable energy and better health lies in minimizing glucose spikes. However, many readers found themselves asking, "How can I take these principles and incorporate them into everyday meals?" This cookbook is the answer to that question, turning theoretical insights into practical, delicious recipes.

The aim of this cookbook is straightforward: to make glucose management not only accessible but enjoyable. It provides recipes that are not only aligned with glucose-stabilizing practices but are also flavorful and diverse, proving that you don't have to compromise taste to support your health. The objective is to offer tools that make it easy for anyone to implement glucose-friendly habits seamlessly into their daily routine, making balanced eating second nature.

Why Glucose Management Matters

To grasp the significance of managing blood sugar, it's crucial to understand glucose's role in the body. Glucose, often termed blood sugar, is the primary energy source for all cells. Whether it's fueling brain function, muscle activity, or organ systems, balanced levels of glucose are vital for optimal function and overall health. Yet, the way we consume and process glucose can greatly affect how it impacts our body.

When we eat foods that are rich in sugar or processed carbohydrates, blood sugar spikes rapidly. In response, the body releases insulin, a hormone that helps store excess glucose. While this process is a natural part of maintaining balance, repeated cycles of high spikes followed by rapid drops can take a toll. They can leave us feeling lethargic, trigger cravings for more sugary foods, and affect our mood stability. Over time, these cycles can contribute to serious health conditions, such as insulin resistance, type 2 diabetes, and chronic inflammation.

Jessie Inchauspe's work emphasizes that glucose stability isn't only important for those with diagnosed blood sugar issues. It's a crucial component for anyone seeking better energy, fewer cravings, and improved mood. This is because glucose has a direct impact on both physical and mental states. By learning how to stabilize glucose levels, we can support a range of health benefits—from reducing midday slumps and brain fog to promoting a balanced metabolism.

This cookbook builds upon Jessie's insights, translating them into tangible recipes that support these benefits. The goal is to show that it's possible to enjoy food and nourish your body in a way that keeps glucose levels balanced, supporting long-term health.

Adapting Science to the Kitchen

The heart of this cookbook lies in taking Jessie's scientifically backed strategies and transforming them into practical, everyday cooking tips and recipes. Understanding the science of glucose is one thing, but translating that knowledge into daily habits is where the challenge lies for many people. This cookbook emphasizes easy-to-implement changes that make a real difference without requiring extreme measures or complex diet plans.

Each recipe has been designed with the intention of making blood sugar management simple and enjoyable. The Glucose Goddess Method focuses on adding beneficial habits rather than imposing restrictive measures. For example, one core practice involves structuring meals in a specific way to support better glucose management. Starting meals with fiber-rich vegetables, followed by protein and healthy fats, and finishing with carbohydrates can reduce the overall glucose spike from the meal. This strategic ordering creates a natural buffer that slows down the absorption of sugar into the bloodstream.

Incorporating these practices into recipes means that you'll find a variety of meal options that align with the Glucose Goddess Method. Whether it's a savory breakfast that sets the tone for balanced energy or a dinner recipe that includes all the components to minimize a post-meal glucose surge, the cookbook is structured to guide you through each step. It's designed to help you make meals that are satisfying, health-supportive, and easy to prepare, ensuring that you can stick to these habits in the long term.

Who Will Benefit from This Cookbook

This cookbook is intended for anyone seeking a better relationship with food and energy. If you frequently experience energy crashes in the middle of the day, struggle with sugar cravings, or find it hard to maintain focus, the recipes in this book can help you regain control. The Glucose Goddess Method is perfect for those looking for a sustainable approach to healthy eating, one where the emphasis is on adding positive, health-supportive practices rather than strict limitations.

Stabilizing blood sugar levels can be transformative, not just for overall energy but also for managing specific health challenges. People dealing with weight management difficulties, hormonal imbalances, or fatigue can benefit from understanding how their body processes glucose. By adopting recipes and techniques inspired by Jessie Inchauspe's teachings, you'll find that taking care of your health doesn't have to mean giving up the foods you love or following complicated diet plans. Instead, it's about making simple, informed choices that align with your body's natural rhythms.

The cookbook aims to serve as a tool that helps you build a foundation for better health without the pressure of drastic measures or extreme dieting. The goal is to make you feel empowered in the kitchen, equipped with the knowledge and recipes to create meals that support steady energy and well-being.

What to Expect from This Book

Within this cookbook, you'll discover a collection of recipes that focus on glucose-friendly eating without sacrificing taste or enjoyment. You'll learn how to create meals that satisfy your cravings while supporting your health goals. Each chapter is designed to guide you through adopting strategies that can make a significant difference in how you feel day to day. Whether it's starting your day with a savory, balanced breakfast or incorporating fiber-rich starters into your meals, the cookbook offers clear explanations and practical recipes that make it easy to get started.

The recipes include a variety of options for different tastes and dietary needs, showing that balanced eating can be both delicious and adaptable. The instructions are straightforward, so whether you're a seasoned cook or someone just beginning to experiment in the kitchen, you'll find guidance that fits your comfort level.

This cookbook is more than just a collection of recipes; it's an invitation to harness the benefits of glucose balance for a more energetic, fulfilling life. It's about small, meaningful changes that bring lasting health benefits. Each meal becomes an opportunity to nourish your body and support your well-being, proving that better health is within reach—one delicious dish at a time.

Chapter 1

Understanding Glucose and Its Effects

Before we delve into the practical methods and recipes, it's essential to understand why managing glucose plays a critical role in overall health. Glucose, often referred to as blood sugar, is the main fuel source for every cell in your body. From powering your brain to enabling muscle movement and supporting essential bodily functions, glucose is at the core of how our bodies generate and use energy. Yet, while our bodies rely on glucose for optimal function, the way it enters and is processed within the body can make a significant difference to our well-being.

The Role of Glucose as an Energy Source

Glucose acts as the body's primary energy source, derived from the foods we eat, particularly carbohydrates. Simple carbohydrates like refined sugars and processed foods break down quickly in the digestive system, releasing glucose into the bloodstream at a rapid pace. Complex carbohydrates, on the other hand, are broken down more slowly, releasing glucose steadily. This difference is where the concept of glucose management becomes important.

When we consume foods that cause a quick surge in blood sugar—such as sweets, baked goods, or sugary drinks—our body responds by releasing insulin, a hormone produced by the pancreas. Insulin helps transport glucose from the blood into cells where it can be used for energy or stored for later use. However, when blood sugar spikes sharply, the body may release a large amount of insulin to bring levels down quickly, often resulting in a significant drop in blood sugar shortly after. This sudden drop can leave you feeling tired, irritable, and craving more sugar as your body seeks to regain energy quickly.

The Impact of Glucose Spikes and Crashes

The cycle of rapid glucose spikes followed by steep crashes is more than just a minor inconvenience; it can have profound effects on both physical and mental health. Initially, a high blood sugar spike may provide a short-lived burst of energy or satisfaction, but the crash that follows can lead to feelings of fatigue, low mood, and increased hunger. These fluctuations in blood sugar don't just impact your energy levels—they set the stage for persistent cravings that drive you to consume more sugary or refined foods, perpetuating the cycle.

Over time, the cumulative effect of these spikes and drops can lead to insulin resistance. In this condition, cells become less responsive to insulin, requiring the pancreas to produce even more of the hormone to manage blood sugar levels. This is a precursor to type 2 diabetes and is often accompanied by other metabolic health issues. But the effects don't stop at physical health. Glucose instability can influence mental well-being as well, contributing to anxiety, mood swings, and even depressive symptoms. The brain requires steady fuel to function optimally, and erratic blood sugar levels can interfere with that process, impacting cognitive function and emotional balance.

Long-Term Health Implications

The consequences of poor glucose management can extend beyond short-term fatigue and mood changes. Chronic blood sugar instability has been linked to an increased risk of developing inflammatory conditions, cardiovascular disease, and metabolic syndrome. The body's inflammatory response can be heightened by frequent blood sugar fluctuations, leading to long-term damage if not addressed.

Jessie Inchauspe's insights emphasize that the impact of glucose management is universal—it isn't only vital for those with diabetes or metabolic disorders. People who frequently experience energy crashes, brain fog, or intense sugar cravings often have underlying blood sugar imbalances, even if they don't have a diagnosed condition. This is why understanding how glucose works and how to manage its effects is crucial for everyone looking to improve their overall health.

The Good News: Managing Glucose for Better Health

The positive takeaway is that glucose management is within reach and doesn't require drastic measures or complicated routines. By learning to stabilize blood sugar levels through dietary and lifestyle changes, you can improve both how you feel and your long-term health outlook. Stabilizing blood sugar means fewer peaks and valleys in energy levels, more consistent moods, and reduced cravings, all of which contribute to a higher quality of life.

In this section of the cookbook, we dive deeper into how glucose affects not just your energy but your entire body's function. You'll learn why stabilizing blood sugar is not just a way to avoid chronic health problems but a strategy for feeling better day-to-day. Through the recipes and practices inspired by Jessie Inchauspe's teachings, this cookbook will show you how to take control of your diet in a way that supports stable glucose levels and promotes long-term well-being.

With a better understanding of how your body processes glucose, you'll be equipped to make informed choices that lead to meaningful, positive changes. This foundation of knowledge empowers you to approach your meals with intention, turning everyday eating into an opportunity for enhanced energy and improved overall health.

Chapter 2

Core Principles and Hacks

At the core of the Glucose Goddess Method is a commitment to simplicity. The idea isn't to burden you with an overwhelming set of rules but to show that small, mindful adjustments in how and when you eat can make a significant difference. Inspired by Jessie Inchauspe's research and practical insights, this cookbook outlines key strategies that are designed to be easily incorporated into daily life. The focus is on creating a set of habits that are not only effective but also sustainable over time, helping you maintain balanced glucose levels without feeling deprived or restricted.

Why Simplicity Works

The beauty of these principles lies in their accessibility. Through years of research and personal exploration, it became evident that dramatic, hard-to-follow changes often lead to quick burnout. Instead, lasting success comes from making minor shifts that add up to major benefits. By implementing straightforward changes in your eating habits, you can support your body's natural processes in a way that is easy to maintain.

These core principles are meant to seamlessly fit into your routine, making the pursuit of balanced blood sugar levels feel natural rather than forced. They aren't based on drastic diet trends or intense restrictions but are rooted in small, scientifically supported practices that work in harmony with your body's needs.

The Power of Food Order: The "Veggie Starter" Hack

One of the standout principles featured in this cookbook is the practice of structuring your meals with a "veggie starter." Research has shown that the order in which you eat your food can significantly influence the way your body processes glucose. Starting your meals with vegetables or other fiber-rich foods helps create a physical barrier in your digestive system, slowing down the absorption of sugars and starches. This approach can substantially reduce the glucose spike that typically follows a meal.

The reason this hack is effective is simple: fiber slows the digestive process, allowing sugars from the rest of the meal to enter your bloodstream more gradually. This not only helps keep your glucose levels steady but also reduces sudden insulin surges that can lead to fatigue and cravings. The "veggie starter" is a practical, achievable habit that can be incorporated into nearly any meal, whether you're at home or dining out.

In this cookbook, you'll find recipes that highlight how to make this practice part of your daily life. From light salads to hearty vegetable dishes that can be enjoyed as the first course, these recipes provide an easy, delicious way to start your meals off right.

The Importance of a Savory Breakfast

Another powerful hack to help manage glucose levels is starting your day with a savory breakfast. The first meal of the day sets the stage for how your body responds to food throughout the day. Many common breakfast choices, such as pastries, cereals, and fruit juices, are high in refined carbohydrates and sugars. These can cause a rapid spike in blood sugar and insulin, triggering the glucose roller coaster that many people experience—highs followed by sudden drops that lead to cravings and low energy.

A savory breakfast that includes proteins, healthy fats, and fiber provides a more balanced start. It helps your body maintain steady glucose levels, which can lead to more consistent energy, reduced hunger, and better focus throughout the day. By opting for meals such as eggs with leafy greens, avocado toast with whole grain bread, or a protein-rich smoothie with minimal sugar, you can support your body's metabolic balance from the moment you wake up.

This cookbook includes a variety of savory breakfast recipes designed to nourish your body and promote stable blood sugar. The goal is to make it easy for you to start your day with foods that satisfy and energize without the inevitable crash that follows sugary breakfasts.

Adding, Not Restricting

One of the most important aspects of the Glucose Goddess Method is that it focuses on addition rather than restriction. Unlike many diet approaches that center around eliminating certain foods or food groups, this method encourages you to add beneficial practices and foods into your meals. You don't need to cut out the foods you love; instead, learn how to enjoy them in a way that supports your body's natural glucose management.

For instance, adding a vegetable starter or a side of protein and healthy fats can buffer the impact of the carbohydrates that follow. These practices allow your body to process your meals more evenly, reducing spikes and helping you feel more satisfied. This approach shifts the mindset from one of deprivation to one of abundance and empowerment. By focusing on what you can add to your meals, you're more likely to maintain these habits and experience the positive changes that come with them.

What This Section Covers

In this section of the cookbook, I have taken you through the core principles and explain how they work in greater detail. You'll have discover how easy it is to integrate these small adjustments into your life and start reaping the benefits. Each principle is supported by recipes and practical tips that illustrate how to put these hacks into action. By now, you'll feel confident in your ability to implement these strategies, supporting your body's natural rhythm and improving your overall well-being.

These hacks are not complicated, nor do they require significant time or effort. They are designed to work with your lifestyle, not against it, ensuring that managing glucose becomes a seamless, enjoyable part of your daily routine.

Chapter 3

Tips for Sustainable Changes

One of the most frequently asked questions is how to make positive changes last over time. Starting any new practice often feels exciting at first, but maintaining that momentum can be challenging. Many people find themselves committed to new habits for a few weeks, only to feel their enthusiasm wane as daily life becomes busy or stressful. This is why the Glucose Goddess Method is not just about teaching you the science behind blood sugar management—it's about showing you how to make these strategies a seamless part of your life.

Emphasizing Consistency Over Perfection

A key principle of this method is understanding that it's not about perfection, but rather about consistency. Sustainable change happens when small habits become second nature. If the idea of managing blood sugar feels daunting or rigid, it's easy to lose motivation. That's why this book emphasizes adaptable, practical advice that fits into the realities of everyday life. Whether you're at home, at work, dining out, or even traveling, these tips will guide you in making better choices without feeling like you have to be perfect all the time.

Consistency doesn't mean you have to follow every tip perfectly or adhere to strict rules. Instead, it means implementing the practices most of the time and giving yourself grace when things don't go as planned. Life is full of unexpected events, from last-minute dinners with friends to busy workdays that leave little time for meal prep. The goal is to build flexibility into your habits so you can stay on track even when life throws you a curveball.

Integrating Glucose Hacks Into Daily Life

The true power of the Glucose Goddess Method lies in its adaptability. It's designed to complement your lifestyle, not complicate it. Here are some of the key tips you'll find in this section that help integrate glucose-friendly practices sustainably:

- **Mindful Meal Planning at Home:** Preparing meals at home provides you with more control over what you're eating. This section will guide you on how to plan meals that naturally incorporate the Glucose Goddess principles, such as starting with fiber-rich vegetables, balancing your meals with protein and healthy fats, and enjoying carbohydrates in a way that minimizes glucose spikes. The recipes in this book are crafted to be easy, enjoyable, and adaptable, so you don't feel restricted.
- **Eating Out with Confidence:** Dining out or ordering takeout doesn't have to derail your glucose management. Simple strategies such as ordering a side salad to start your meal, choosing dishes with lean proteins and veggies, and making small adjustments like asking for sauces on the side can help you keep your blood sugar steady without missing out on social events or favorite foods. This book provides practical tips for navigating menus and making informed decisions that align with your goals.
- **On-the-Go Snacking:** Busy days often call for quick solutions, and it's easy to grab whatever is convenient when you're hungry and on the move. This section will introduce you to glucose-friendly snack options and simple swaps that are easy to keep on hand, such as nuts, hummus with vegetables, or a boiled egg. These choices provide nourishment without causing sharp blood sugar spikes, helping you stay energized between meals.
- **Adapting the Method to Your Routine:** Every person's schedule is different, which is why flexibility is essential. Whether you're a parent managing meals for the whole family, a professional balancing work with healthy eating, or someone who travels frequently, the tips here are adaptable. They show you how to tweak your approach to align with whatever life stage or lifestyle you have, making glucose-friendly eating realistic and sustainable.

Motivation to Keep Going

Maintaining any new habit requires a source of motivation that reinforces why you're making the change in the first place. This section of the book is designed to keep you inspired by sharing the positive outcomes that come with consistency. Even if the progress feels gradual, each small step helps build a foundation of better health and well-being. By focusing on how these practices improve your energy, reduce cravings, and support a balanced mood, you'll find motivation in the benefits you experience over time.

It's also important to acknowledge that setbacks happen. The Glucose Goddess Method isn't about all-or-nothing thinking; it's about building a relationship with food and health that feels sustainable. If you have days when you don't follow the hacks perfectly, that's okay. What matters is getting back on track and continuing to make choices that align with your health goals. This mindset shift from rigid adherence to flexible consistency is what makes these changes last.

Building a Foundation for Long-Term Success

The ultimate goal of this section is to equip you with the tools and mindset needed to build sustainable, healthy habits. The tips outlined in this book will help you make glucose-friendly choices feel intuitive, regardless of where you are or what you're doing. It's about creating a balanced approach that fits into your life seamlessly, ensuring that glucose management becomes a habit rather than an obligation.

By following these strategies most of the time, you'll notice improvements that reinforce your commitment to this journey. Sustainable change is built on consistency, small wins, and the flexibility to adapt when needed. This section of the book aims to guide you in finding your rhythm and enjoying the journey toward a more balanced, healthier life.

The Glucose Goddess Recipes

Coconut and Berry Smoothie

Prep time: 5 minutes | Cook time: 0 minutes | Serves 2

Ingredients
- ½ cup mixed berries (blueberries, strawberries, blackberries)
- 1 tablespoon ground flaxseed
- 2 tablespoons unsweetened coconut flakes
- ½ cup unsweetened plain coconut milk
- ½ cup leafy greens (kale, spinach)
- ¼ cup unsweetened vanilla nonfat yogurt
- ½ cup ice

Directions
- The berries, flaxseed, coconut flakes, coconut milk, greens, yogurt, and ice should all be combined in a blender jar.
- Process till it's smooth. Serve.

Per Serving
calories: 182 | fat: 14.9g | protein: 5.9g | carbs: 8.1g | fiber: 4.1g | sugar: 2.9g | sodium: 25mg

Walnut and Oat Granola

Prep time: 10 minutes | Cook time: 30 minutes | Serves 16

Ingredients
- 4 cups rolled oats
- 1 cup walnut pieces
- ½ cup pepitas
- ¼ teaspoon salt
- 1 teaspoon ground cinnamon
- 1 teaspoon ground ginger
- ½ cup coconut oil, melted
- ½ cup unsweetened applesauce
- 1 teaspoon vanilla extract
- ½ cup dried cherries

Directions
- Set the oven's temperature to 350°F (180°C). Put parchment paper on a baking pan.
- Combine the oats, pepitas, walnuts, salt, cinnamon, and ginger in a big bowl.
- Put the applesauce, vanilla, and coconut oil in a large measuring cup. After adding the dry mixture, thoroughly mix.
- Pour the mixture onto the baking sheet that has been prepared. Cook, stirring halfway through, for 30 minutes. Take the granola out of the oven and leave it alone until it cools fully. Add the dried cherries after breaking the granola into bits.
- Store for up to two weeks at room temperature after transferring to an airtight container.

Per Serving
calories: 225 | fat: 14.9g | protein: 4.9g | carbs: 20.1g | fiber: 3.1g | sugar: 4.9g | sodium: 31mg

Crispy Pita with Canadian Bacon

Prep time: 5 minutes | Cook time: 15 minutes | Serves 2

Ingredients
- 1 (6-inch) whole-grain pita bread
- 3 teaspoons extra-virgin olive oil, divided
- 2 eggs
- 2 Canadian bacon slices
- Juice of ½ lemon
- 1 cup microgreens
- 2 tablespoons crumbled goat cheese
- Freshly ground black pepper, to taste

Directions
- A big skillet should be heated to medium heat. Divide the pita bread in half, then use ¼ teaspoon of olive oil on each side of each half, for a total of 1 teaspoon of oil. Remove from the skillet after cooking for 2 to 3 minutes on each side.
- Heat 1 teaspoon of oil in the same skillet over medium heat. Cook the eggs in the skillet for two to three minutes, or until they are set. Take out of the skillet.
- Cook the Canadian bacon in the same skillet, turning once, for 3 to 5 minutes.
- Whisk the lemon juice and the remaining 1 teaspoon of oil together in a large bowl. Toss to incorporate the microgreens.
- Place half of the microgreens, one piece of bacon, one egg, and one tablespoon of goat cheese on top of each pita half. Add pepper for seasoning, then serve.

Per Serving
calories: 251 | fat: 13.9g | protein: 13.1g | carbs: 20.1g | fiber: 3.1g | sugar: 0.9g | sodium: 400mg

Coconut and Chia Pudding

Prep time: 5 minutes | Cook time: 0 minutes | Serves 2

Ingredients
- 7 ounces (198 g) light coconut milk
- ¼ cup chia seeds
- 3 to 4 drops liquid stevia
- 1 clementine
- 1 kiwi
- Shredded coconut (unsweetened)

Directions
- To begin, place the light coconut milk in a mixing dish. To make the milk sweeter, add the liquid stevia. Stir thoroughly.
- Whisk the chia seeds into the milk until they are thoroughly mixed. Put aside.
- Carefully remove the clementine's skin from the wedges after peeling it. Put aside.
- Additionally, cut the kiwi into little pieces after peeling it.
- Fill a glass jar with the pudding. Put the fruits to the bottom of the jar and top it up with a scoop of chia pudding. Spread the fruits now, and then cover with more chia pudding.
- Add the remaining fruits and shredded coconut as a final garnish.

Per Serving
calories: 486 | fat: 40.5g | protein: 8.5g | carbs: 30.8g | fiber: 15.6g | sugar: 11.6g | sodium: 24mg

Blueberry Muffins

Prep time: 10 minutes | Cook time: 25 minutes | Serves 18 muffins

Ingredients
- 2 cups whole-wheat pastry flour
- 1 cup almond flour
- ½ cup granulated sweetener
- 1 tablespoon baking powder
- 2 teaspoons freshly grated lemon zest
- ¾ teaspoon baking soda
- ¾ teaspoon ground nutmeg
- Pinch sea salt
- 2 eggs
- 1 cup skim milk, at room temperature
- ¾ cup 2 percent plain Greek yogurt
- ½ cup melted coconut oil
- 1 tablespoon freshly squeezed lemon juice
- 1 teaspoon pure vanilla extract
- 1 cup fresh blueberries

Directions
- Set the oven's temperature to 350°F (180°C).
- Place paper liners inside 18 muffin cups and place the tray aside.
- Mix the flour, almond flour, baking powder, sweetener, baking soda, nutmeg, salt, and lemon zest in a big bowl.
- Whisk the eggs, milk, yogurt, coconut oil, lemon juice, and vanilla in a small bowl.
- Stir just until mixed after adding the wet components to the dry ingredients.
- Don't crush the blueberries; just fold them in.
- Evenly spoon the batter into each muffin cup. Bake the muffins for about 25 minutes, or until a toothpick inserted in the center comes out clean.
- Serve the muffins after they have fully cooled.
- Remaining muffins can be frozen for up to a month or kept in the fridge for up to three days in an airtight container.

Per Serving
calories: 166 | fat: 9.1g | protein: 3.9g | carbs: 18.1g | fiber: 2.1g | sugar: 6.9g | sodium: 75mg

Apple and Bran Muffins

Prep time: 10 minutes | Cook time: 20 minutes | Makes 18 muffins

---

Ingredients
- 2 cups whole-wheat flour
- 1 cup wheat bran
- ⅓ cup granulated sweetener
- 1 tablespoon baking powder
- 2 teaspoons ground cinnamon
- ½ teaspoon ground ginger
- ¼ teaspoon ground nutmeg
- Pinch sea salt
- 2 eggs
- 1½ cups skim milk, at room temperature
- ½ cup melted coconut oil
- 2 teaspoons pure vanilla extract
- 2 apples, peeled, cored, and diced

Directions
- Set the oven's temperature to 350°F (180°C).
- Place paper liners inside 18 muffin cups and place the tray aside.
- Mix the flour, bran, baking powder, sweetener, cinnamon, ginger, nutmeg, and salt in a big bowl.
- Whisk together the eggs, milk, coconut oil, and vanilla in a small bowl.
- Stirring just until mixed, add the wet components to the dry ingredients.
- Spoon equal amounts of batter into each muffin cup and stir in the apples.
- Bake the muffins for about 20 minutes, or until a toothpick inserted in the middle of one comes out clean.
- Serve the muffins after they have fully cooled.
- Remaining muffins can be frozen for up to a month or kept in the fridge for up to three days in an airtight container.

Per Serving
calories: 142 | fat: 7.1g | protein: 4.1g | carbs: 19.1g | fiber: 3.1g | sugar: 6.1g | sodium: 21mg

Coconut and Berry Oatmeal

Prep time: 10 minutes | Cook time: 35 minutes | Serves 6

Ingredients

- 2 cups rolled oats
- ¼ cup shredded unsweetened coconut
- 1 teaspoon baking powder
- ½ teaspoon ground cinnamon
- ¼ teaspoon sea salt
- 2 cups skim milk
- ¼ cup melted coconut oil, plus extra for greasing the baking dish
- 1 egg
- 1 teaspoon pure vanilla extract
- 2 cups fresh blueberries
- ⅛ cup chopped pecans, for garnish
- 1 teaspoon chopped fresh mint leaves, for garnish

Directions

- Set the oven's temperature to 350°F (180°C).
- Set aside a baking dish that has been lightly oiled.
- Combine the oats, coconut, baking powder, cinnamon, and salt in a medium-sized bowl.
- Mix the milk, oil, egg, and vanilla in a small bowl with a whisk until thoroughly combined.
- In the baking dish, arrange half of the dry ingredients, then half of the berries. Then, spread the remaining half of the dry ingredients and the remaining berries on top.
- Evenly fill the baking dish with the wet ingredients. To distribute the wet ingredients evenly, give it a little tap on the counter.
- Cover and bake the dish for about 35 minutes, or until the oats are soft.
- Garnish with the pecans and mint and serve right away.

Per Serving

calories: 296 | fat: 17.1g | protein: 10.2g | carbs: 26.9g | fiber: 4.1g | sugar: 10.9g | sodium: 154mg

Spanakopita Frittata

Prep time: 10 minutes | Cook time: 15 minutes | Serves 4

Ingredients

- 2 tablespoons extra-virgin olive oil
- ½ sweet onion, chopped
- 1 red bell pepper, seeded and chopped
- ½ teaspoon minced garlic
- ¼ teaspoon sea salt
- ½ teaspoon freshly ground black pepper
- 8 egg whites
- 2 cups shredded spinach
- ½ cup crumbled low-sodium feta cheese
- 1 teaspoon chopped fresh parsley, for garnish

Directions

- Set the oven temperature to 375°F (190°C).
- Heat the olive oil in a heavy ovenproof skillet over medium-high heat.
- For around five minutes, sauté the bell pepper, onion, and garlic until they are tender. Add salt and pepper for seasoning.
- In a medium bowl, whisk the egg whites together. Then, pour the egg whites into the skillet and shake the pan gently to distribute them.
- Without stirring, cook the eggs and vegetables for three minutes.
- Evenly distribute the feta cheese on top of the spinach after scattering it over the eggs.
- Place the skillet in the oven and bake it uncovered for around ten minutes, or until it is cooked through and firm.
- Using a rubber spatula, loosen the frittata's edges and flip it over onto a platter.
- Serve after adding the chopped parsley as a garnish.

Per Serving

calories: 146 | fat: 10.1g | protein: 10.1g | carbs: 3.9g | fiber: 1.0g | sugar: 2.9g | sodium: 292mg

Ratatouille Egg Bake

Prep time: 20 minutes | Cook time: 50 minutes | Serves 4

Ingredients

- 2 teaspoons extra-virgin olive oil
- ½ sweet onion, finely chopped
- 2 teaspoons minced garlic
- ½ small eggplant, peeled and diced
- 1 green zucchini, diced
- 1 yellow zucchini, diced
- 1 red bell pepper, seeded and diced
- 3 tomatoes, seeded and chopped
- 1 tablespoon chopped fresh oregano
- 1 tablespoon chopped fresh basil
- Pinch red pepper flakes
- Sea salt and freshly ground black pepper, to taste
- 4 large eggs

Directions

- Set the oven's temperature to 350°F (180°C).
- Add the olive oil to a large ovenproof skillet and place it over medium heat.
- For around three minutes, sauté the onion and garlic until they are tender and transparent. Add the eggplant and cook, stirring periodically, for approximately ten minutes. Add the pepper and zucchini, then cook for five minutes.
- Cover and lower the heat to low. Simmer for 15 minutes or until the vegetables are tender.
- Cook for an additional 10 minutes after adding the tomatoes, oregano, basil, and red pepper flakes. Add salt and pepper to the ratatouille.
- Make four wells in the mixture using a spoon. In each well, crack an egg.
- Put the pan in the oven and bake it for about five minutes, or until the eggs are set.
- Take it out of the oven. Accompany the eggs with a heaping portion of veggies.

Per Serving

calories: 148 | fat: 7.9g | protein: 9.1g | carbs: 13.1g | fiber: 4.1g | sugar: 7.1g | sodium: 99mg

Cottage Pancakes

Prep time: 10 minutes | Cook time: 20 minutes | Serves 4

Ingredients
- 2 cups low-fat cottage cheese
- 4 egg whites
- 2 eggs
- 1 tablespoon pure vanilla extract
- 1½ cups almond flour
- Nonstick cooking spray

Directions
- In a blender, pulse together the cottage cheese, eggs, egg whites, and vanilla.
- In the blender, add the almond flour and process until it's smooth.
- Apply a thin layer of cooking spray to a big nonstick skillet and place it over medium heat.
- Four pancakes at a time, spoon ¼ cup of batter into the griddle.
- Cook the pancakes for about 4 minutes, or until the bottoms are brown and firm.
- Cook the pancakes for approximately three minutes on the other side, or until they are cooked through.
- Repeat with the remaining batter after removing the pancakes to a platter.
- Accompany the dish with fresh fruit.

Per Serving
calories: 345 | fat: 22.1g | protein: 29.1g | carbs: 11.1g | fiber: 4.1g | sugar: 5.1g | sodium: 560mg

Greek Yogurt and Oat Pancakes

Prep time: 5 minutes | Cook time: 20 minutes | Serves 4

Ingredients

- 1 cup 2 percent plain Greek yogurt
- 3 eggs
- 1½ teaspoons pure vanilla extract
- 1 cup rolled oats
- 1 tablespoon granulated sweetener
- 1 teaspoon baking powder
- 1 teaspoon ground cinnamon
- Pinch ground cloves
- Nonstick cooking spray

Directions

- In a blender, add the yogurt, eggs, and vanilla; pulse to mix.
- In the blender, combine the oats, baking powder, cloves, cinnamon, and sweetener. Blend until the mixture is smooth.
- Lightly spray cooking spray on a big nonstick skillet and place it over medium heat.
- Four pancakes at a time, spoon ¼ cup of batter into the griddle.
- Cook the pancakes for about 4 minutes, or until the bottoms are brown and firm.
- Cook the pancakes for approximately three minutes on the other side, or until they are cooked through.
- Repeat with the remaining batter after removing the pancakes to a platter.
- Accompany the dish with fresh fruit.

Per Serving

calories: 244 | fat: 8.1g | protein: 13.1g | carbs: 28.1g | fiber: 4.0g | sugar: 3.0g | sodium: 82mg

Apple and Pumpkin Waffles

Prep time: 10 minutes | Cook time: 20 minutes | Serves 6

Ingredients
- 2¼ cups whole-wheat pastry flour
- 2 tablespoons granulated sweetener
- 1 tablespoon baking powder
- 1 teaspoon ground cinnamon
- 1 teaspoon ground nutmeg
- 4 eggs
- 1¼ cups pure pumpkin purée
- 1 apple, peeled, cored, and finely chopped
- Melted coconut oil, for cooking

Directions
- Mix the flour, baking powder, cinnamon, nutmeg, and sweetener in a big bowl.
- Whisk the eggs and pumpkin together in a small bowl.
- Whisk together the wet and dry components until they are smooth.
- Add the apple to the batter and stir.
- Brush your waffle iron with melted coconut oil and cook the waffles as directed by the waffle maker manufacturer until all of the batter has been used.
- Serve right away.

Per Serving
calories: 232 | fat: 4.1g | protein: 10.9g | carbs: 40.1g | fiber: 7.1g | sugar: 5.1g | sodium: 52mg

Buckwheat Crêpes

Prep time: 20 minutes | Cook time: 20 minutes | Serves 5

Ingredients

- 1½ cups skim milk
- 3 eggs
- 1 teaspoon extra-virgin olive oil, plus more for the skillet
- 1 cup buckwheat flour
- ½ cup whole-wheat flour
- ½ cup 2 percent plain Greek yogurt
- 1 cup sliced strawberries
- 1 cup blueberries

Directions

- Whisk the eggs, milk, and 1 teaspoon oil in a large bowl until thoroughly blended.
- Sift the whole-wheat and buckwheat flours into a medium basin. Whisk the dry components into the wet ingredients until they are smooth and completely blended.
- Before cooking, let the batter rest for at least two hours.
- Lightly grease the bottom of a big skillet or crêpe pan and place it over medium-high heat.
- Fill the skillet with approximately ¼ cup of batter. Until the batter covers the bottom of the pan, swirl it around.
- After approximately a minute of cooking, turn the crêpe over. Cook until the crêpe is gently browned, about 1 minute more on the opposite side. To keep warm, move the cooked crêpe to a platter and cover with a fresh dish towel.
- Continue until all of the batter has been utilized; roughly ten crêpes should result.
- Put two crêpes on each plate and spoon 1 tablespoon of yogurt onto each one.
- Serve with berries on top.

Per Serving (2 Crêpes)
calories: 330 | fat: 6.9g | protein: 15.9g | carbs: 54.1g | fiber: 7.9g | sugar: 11.1g | sodium: 100mg

Mushroom Frittata

Prep time: 10 minutes | Cook time: 15 minutes | Serves 4

Ingredients
- 8 large eggs
- ½ cup skim milk
- ¼ teaspoon ground nutmeg
- Sea salt and freshly ground black pepper, to taste
- 2 teaspoons extra-virgin olive oil
- 2 cups sliced wild mushrooms (cremini, oyster, shiitake, portobello, etc.)
- ½ red onion, chopped
- 1 teaspoon minced garlic
- ½ cup goat cheese, crumbled

Directions
- Turn the broiler on.
- Whisk the eggs, milk, and nutmeg together in a medium-sized bowl until thoroughly blended. Set aside the egg mixture after lightly seasoning it with salt and pepper.
- Oil should be added to an ovenproof skillet over medium heat, turning the pan to fully coat the bottom.
- For around seven minutes, sauté the garlic, onion, and mushrooms until they become transparent.
- Lift the edges of the cooked egg to let the uncooked egg seep underneath, then pour the egg mixture into the skillet and heat until the bottom of the frittata is set.
- Put the skillet in the broiler for approximately one minute, or until the top is set.
- After adding the goat cheese to the frittata, broil it for a further minute or so, or until it melts.
- Take it out of the oven. To serve, cut into 4 wedges.

Per Serving
calories: 227 | fat: 15.1g | protein: 17.1g | carbs: 5.1g | fiber: 0.9g | sugar: 4.1g | sodium: 224mg

Tropical Yogurt Kiwi Bowl

Prep time: 5 minutes | Cook time: 0 minutes | Serves 2

Ingredients
- 1½ cups plain low-fat Greek yogurt
- 2 kiwis, peeled and sliced
- 2 tablespoons shredded unsweetened coconut flakes
- 2 tablespoons halved walnuts
- 1 tablespoon chia seeds
- 2 teaspoons honey, divided (optional)

Directions
- Separate the yogurt into two little dishes.
- Place half of the kiwi slices, coconut flakes, walnuts, chia seeds, and honey (if using) on top of each serving of yogurt.

Per Serving

calories: 261 | fat: 9.1g | protein: 21.1g | carbs: 23.1g | fiber: 6.1g | sugar: 14.1g | sodium: 84mg

Enchilada Black Bean Casserole

Prep time: 15 minutes | Cook time: 15 minutes | Serves 6

Ingredients
- 1 tablespoon extra-virgin olive oil
- ½ onion, chopped
- ½ red bell pepper, seeded and chopped
- ½ green bell pepper, seeded and chopped
- 2 small zucchini, chopped
- 3 garlic cloves, minced
- 1 (15-ounce / 425-g) can low-sodium black beans, drained and rinsed
- 1 (10-ounce / 283-g) can low-sodium enchilada sauce
- 1 teaspoon ground cumin
- ¼ teaspoon salt
- ¼ teaspoon freshly ground black pepper
- ½ cup shredded Cheddar cheese, divided
- 2 (6-inch) corn tortillas, cut into strips
- Chopped fresh cilantro, for garnish
- Plain yogurt, for serving

Directions
- Turn the broiler up to high heat.
- Heat the oil in a large ovenproof skillet over medium-high heat.
- Cook the onion in the skillet for 3 to 5 minutes, or until it softens, after adding the red and green bell peppers, zucchini, and garlic.
- Stir in the black beans, tortilla strips, enchilada sauce, cumin, salt, pepper, and ¼ cup of cheese. Add the remaining ¼ cup of cheese on top.
- The cheese should be melted and bubbling after 5 to 8 minutes of broiling the skillet. Serve with yogurt on the side and garnish with cilantro.

Per Serving
calories: 172 | fat: 7.1g | protein: 8.1g | carbs: 20.9g | fiber: 6.9g | sugar: 3.0g | sodium: 566mg

Crispy Parmesan Bean and Veggie Cups

Prep time: 10 minutes | **Cook time:** 5 minutes | **Serves 4**

Ingredients

- 1 cup grated Parmesan cheese, divided
- 1 (15-ounce / 425-g) can low-sodium white beans, drained and rinsed
- 1 cucumber, peeled and finely diced
- ½ cup finely diced red onion
- ¼ cup thinly sliced fresh basil
- 1 garlic clove, minced
- ½ jalapeño pepper, diced
- 1 tablespoon extra-virgin olive oil
- 1 tablespoon balsamic vinegar
- ¼ teaspoon salt
- Freshly ground black pepper, to taste

Directions

- A medium nonstick skillet should be heated to medium heat. Using a spatula, flatten two tablespoons of cheese into a thin circle in the middle of the pan.
- Once the cheese has melted, turn it over with a spatula and lightly brown the other side.
- After taking the cheese "pancake" out of the pan, carefully bend it with your hands to fit inside the muffin tin.
- Continue until you have eight cups of cheese.
- Add the beans, cucumber, onion, garlic, jalapeño, basil, olive oil, vinegar, and salt and pepper to a mixing bowl.
- Just before serving, pour the bean mixture into each cup.

Per Serving

calories: 260 | fat: 12.1g | protein: 14.9 | carbs: 23.9g | fiber: 8.0g | sugar: 3.9g | sodium: 552mg

Green Lentils with Summer Vegetables

Prep time: 15 minutes | Cook time: 0 minutes | Serves 4

Ingredients
- 3 tablespoons extra-virgin olive oil
- 2 tablespoons balsamic vinegar
- 2 teaspoons chopped fresh basil
- 1 teaspoon minced garlic
- Sea salt and freshly ground black pepper, to taste
- 2 (15-ounce / 425-g) cans sodium-free green lentils, rinsed and drained
- ½ English cucumber, diced
- 2 tomatoes, diced
- ½ cup halved Kalamata olives
- ¼ cup chopped fresh chives
- 2 tablespoons pine nuts

Directions
- In a medium bowl, whisk together the olive oil, vinegar, garlic, and basil. Add salt and pepper for seasoning.
- Add the chives, olives, tomatoes, cucumber, and lentils and stir.
- Serve after adding the pine nuts on top.

Per Serving
calories: 400 | fat: 15.1g | protein: 19.8g | carbs: 48.8g | fiber: 18.8g | sugar: 7.1g | sodium: 439mg

Herbed Beans and Brown Rice Bowl

Prep time: 15 minutes | Cook time: 15 minutes | Serves 8

Ingredients

- 2 teaspoons extra-virgin olive oil
- ½ sweet onion, chopped
- 1 teaspoon minced jalapeño pepper
- 1 teaspoon minced garlic
- 1 (15-ounce / 425-g) can sodium-free red kidney beans, rinsed and drained
- 1 large tomato, chopped
- 1 teaspoon chopped fresh thyme
- Sea salt and freshly ground black pepper, to taste
- 2 cups cooked brown rice

Directions

- Add the olive oil to a big skillet and place it over medium-high heat.
- Sauté the garlic, onion, and jalapeño for around three minutes, or until they are tender.
- Add the tomato, thyme, and beans and stir.
- Cook for around ten minutes, or until thoroughly cooked. Add salt and pepper for seasoning.
- Warm brown rice should be served on top.

Per Serving

calories: 200 | fat: 2.1g | protein: 9.1g | carbs: 37.1g | fiber: 6.1g | sugar: 2.0g | sodium: 40mg

Blueberry Wild Rice

Prep time: 15 minutes | Cook time: 45 minutes | Serves 4

Ingredients
- 1 tablespoon extra-virgin olive oil
- ½ sweet onion, chopped
- 2½ cups sodium-free chicken broth
- 1 cup wild rice, rinsed and drained
- Pinch sea salt
- ½ cup toasted pumpkin seeds
- ½ cup blueberries
- 1 teaspoon chopped fresh basil

Directions
- Add the oil to a medium saucepan and place it over medium-high heat.
- The onion should be tender and transparent after about three minutes of sautéing.
- Bring to a boil after stirring in the broth.
- After adding the rice and salt, turn the heat down to low. For around forty minutes, or until the rice is tender, cover and simmer.
- If necessary, drain off any extra broth. Add the basil, blueberries, and pumpkin seeds and stir.
- Warm up and serve.

Per Serving
calories: 259 | fat: 9.1g | protein: 10.8g | carbs: 37.1g | fiber: 3.9g | sugar: 4.1g | sodium: 543mg

Mushroom Rice with Hazelnut

Prep time: 20 minutes | Cook time: 35 minutes | Serves 8

Ingredients

- 1 tablespoon extra-virgin olive oil
- 1 cup chopped button mushrooms
- ½ sweet onion, chopped
- 1 celery stalk, chopped
- 2 teaspoons minced garlic
- 2 cups brown basmati rice
- 4 cups low-sodium chicken broth
- 1 teaspoon chopped fresh thyme
- Sea salt and freshly ground black pepper, to taste
- ½ cup chopped hazelnuts

Directions

- Add the oil to a big saucepan and place it over medium-high heat.
- For around ten minutes, sauté the garlic, onion, celery, and mushrooms until they are just beginning to brown.
- Sauté for one more minute after adding the rice.
- Bring to a boil after adding the chicken broth.
- Cover the saucepan and lower the heat to low. Simmer for about 20 minutes, or until the rice is soft and the liquid has been absorbed.
- Add salt and pepper to taste and stir in the thyme.
- Add the hazelnuts on top, then serve.

Per Serving
calories: 240 | fat: 6.1g | protein: 7.1g | carbs: 38.9g | fiber: 0.9g | sugar: 1.1g | sodium: 388mg

Barley Kale and Squash Risotto

Prep time: 10 minutes | Cook time: 15 minutes | Serves 6

Ingredients
- 1 teaspoon extra-virgin olive oil
- ½ sweet onion, finely chopped
- 1 teaspoon minced garlic
- 2 cups cooked barley
- 2 cups chopped kale
- 2 cups cooked butternut squash, cut into ½-inch cubes
- 2 tablespoons chopped pistachios
- 1 tablespoon chopped fresh thyme
- Sea salt, to taste

Directions
- Add the oil to a big skillet and place it over medium heat.
- For around three minutes, sauté the onion and garlic until they are tender and transparent.
- After adding the barley and kale, stir for around seven minutes, or until the grains are thoroughly heated and the greens have wilted.
- Add the pistachios, thyme, and squash and stir.
- Add salt and cook until the dish is heated, about 4 minutes.

Per Serving
calories: 160 | fat: 1.9g | protein: 5.1g | carbs: 32.1g | fiber: 7.0g | sugar: 2.0g | sodium: 63mg

Eggplant and Bulgur Pilaf

Prep time: 10 minutes | Cook time: 60 minutes | Serves 4

Ingredients
- 1 tablespoon extra-virgin olive oil
- ½ sweet onion, chopped
- 2 teaspoons minced garlic
- 1 cup chopped eggplant
- 1½ cups bulgur
- 4 cups low-sodium chicken broth
- 1 cup diced tomato
- Sea salt and freshly ground black pepper, to taste
- 2 tablespoons chopped fresh basil

Directions
- A big saucepan should be placed over medium-high heat. After adding the oil, sauté the garlic and onion for about three minutes, or until they are tender and transparent.
- Add the eggplant and cook for 4 minutes to make it soft.
- Add the tomatoes, broth, and bulgur and stir. Heat the mixture until it boils.
- Simmer for around 50 minutes, or until the water has been absorbed, after lowering the heat to low and covering.
- Add salt and pepper to the pilaf.
- Serve after adding the basil as a garnish.

Per Serving
calories: 300 | fat: 4.0g | protein: 14.0g | carbs: 54.0g | fiber: 12.0g | sugar: 7.0g | sodium: 358mg

Couscous with Balsamic Dressing

Prep time: 10 minutes | Cook time: 5 minutes | Serves 6

Ingredients

For the Dressing:
- ¼ cup extra-virgin olive oil
- 2 tablespoons balsamic vinegar
- 1 teaspoon honey
- Sea salt and freshly ground black pepper, to taste

For the Couscous:
- 1¼ cups whole-wheat couscous
- Pinch sea salt
- 1 teaspoon butter
- 2 cups boiling water
- 1 scallion, white and green parts, chopped
- ½ cup chopped pecans
- 2 tablespoons chopped fresh parsley

Directions

To Prepare the Dressing
- Mix the oil, vinegar, and honey with a whisk.
- Add salt and pepper for seasoning, then put aside.

How the Couscous Is Made
- In a large heatproof bowl, combine the couscous, butter, and salt. Then, cover with boiling water. Cover the basin and stir. Give it five minutes to sit. Using a fork, uncover and fluff the couscous.
- Add the parsley, pecans, scallion, and dressing and stir.
- Warm up and serve.

Per Serving

calories: 250 | fat: 12.9g | protein: 5.1g | carbs: 30.1g | fiber: 2.2g | sugar: 1.1g | sodium: 77mg

Quinoa and Lush Vegetable Bowl

Prep time: 15 minutes | Cook time: 15 minutes | Serves 6

Ingredients
- 2 cups vegetable broth
- 1 cup quinoa, well rinsed and drained
- 1 teaspoon extra-virgin olive oil
- ½ sweet onion, chopped
- 2 teaspoons minced garlic
- ½ large green zucchini, halved lengthwise and cut into half disks
- 1 red bell pepper, seeded and cut into thin strips
- 1 cup fresh or frozen corn kernels
- 1 teaspoon chopped fresh basil
- Sea salt and freshly ground black pepper, to taste

Directions
- Add the veggie broth to a medium saucepan set over medium heat. Add the quinoa and bring the liquid to a boil. Turn the heat down to low and cover.
- Cook for about 15 minutes, or until the quinoa has absorbed all of the broth. Take it off the stove and let it to cool a little.
- Put the oil in a large skillet over medium-high heat while the quinoa cooks.
- Sauté the garlic and onion for around three minutes, or until they are tender and transparent.
- Add the corn, bell pepper, and zucchini, and cook for about five minutes, or until the vegetables are crisp-tender.
- Take the skillet off of the burner. Stir the cooked quinoa and the basil together in the skillet. Add salt and pepper for seasoning, then serve.

Per Serving
calories: 159 | fat: 3.0g | protein: 7.1g | carbs: 26.1g | fiber: 2.9g | sugar: 3.0g | sodium: 300mg

Easy Coconut Quinoa

Prep time: 15 minutes | Cook time: 25 minutes | Serves 4

Ingredients

- 2 teaspoons extra-virgin olive oil
- 1 sweet onion, chopped
- 1 tablespoon grated fresh ginger
- 2 teaspoons minced garlic
- 1 cup low-sodium chicken broth
- 1 cup coconut milk
- 1 cup quinoa, well rinsed and drained
- Sea salt, to taste
- ¼ cup shredded, unsweetened coconut

Directions

- Add the oil to a big saucepan and place it over medium-high heat.
- For around three minutes, sauté the garlic, ginger, and onion until they are tender.
- Add the quinoa, coconut milk, and chicken broth.
- After bringing the mixture to a boil, lower the heat and cover. For about 20 minutes, or until the quinoa is soft and most of the liquid has been absorbed, simmer it, stirring now and again.
- Sprinkle salt over the quinoa and serve with the coconut on top.

Per Serving
calories: 355 | fat: 21.1g | protein: 9.1g | carbs: 35.1g | fiber: 6.1g | sugar: 4.0g | sodium: 33mg

Linguine with Kale Pesto

Prep time: 10 minutes | Cook time: 20 minutes | Serves 6

Ingredients
- ½ cup shredded kale
- ½ cup fresh basil
- ½ cup sun-dried tomatoes
- ¼ cup chopped almonds
- 2 tablespoons extra-virgin olive oil
- 8 ounces (227 g) dry whole-wheat linguine
- ½ cup grated Parmesan cheese

Directions
- In a food processor or blender, combine the kale, basil, sun-dried tomatoes, almonds, and olive oil. Pulse for approximately two minutes, or until a chunky paste forms. Transfer the pesto to a bowl and leave it there.
- Turn up the heat to high and bring a big saucepan of water to a boil.
- As directed on the package, cook the pasta until it's al dente.
- After draining, combine the pasta with the Parmesan cheese and pesto.
- Serve right away.

Per Serving
calories: 218 | fat: 10.1g | protein: 9.1g | carbs: 25.1g | fiber: 1.1g | sugar: 2.9g | sodium: 195mg

Lemon Wax Beans

Prep time: 5 minutes | Cook time: 15 minutes | Serves 4

Ingredients
- 2 pounds (907 g) wax beans
- 2 tablespoons extra-virgin olive oil
- Sea salt and freshly ground black pepper, to taste
- Juice of ½ lemon

Directions
- Set the oven's temperature to 400°F (205°C).
- Use aluminum foil to line a baking sheet.
- Combine the beans and olive oil in a big bowl. Add a little salt and pepper for seasoning.
- Spread out the beans after transferring them to the baking pan.
- Roast the beans for 10 to 12 minutes, or until they are soft and caramelized.
- Pour the lemon juice over the beans after transferring them to a serving plate.

Per Serving
calories: 99 | fat: 7.1g | protein: 2.1g | carbs: 8.1g | fiber: 4.2g | sugar: 3.9g | sodium: 814mg

Navy Bean Pico de Gallo

Prep time: 20 minutes | Cook time: 0 minutes | Serves 4

Ingredients
- 2½ cups cooked navy beans
- 1 tomato, diced
- ½ red bell pepper, seeded and chopped
- ¼ jalapeño pepper, chopped
- 1 scallion, white and green parts, chopped
- 1 teaspoon minced garlic
- 1 teaspoon ground cumin
- ½ teaspoon ground coriander
- ½ cup low-sodium feta cheese

Directions
- In a medium bowl, combine the beans, tomato, bell pepper, jalapeño, scallion, garlic, cumin, and coriander, and stir until thoroughly combined.
- Serve after adding the feta cheese on top.

Per Serving

calories: 225 | fat: 4.1g | protein: 14.1g | carbs: 34.1g | fiber: 13.1g | sugar: 3.9g | sodium: 165mg

Tomato and Navy Bean Bake

Prep time: 10 minutes | Cook time: 25 minutes | Serves 8

Ingredients
- 1 teaspoon extra-virgin olive oil
- ½ sweet onion, chopped
- 2 teaspoons minced garlic
- 2 sweet potatoes, peeled and diced
- 1 (28-ounce / 794-g) can low-sodium diced tomatoes
- ¼ cup sodium-free tomato paste
- 2 tablespoons granulated sweetener
- 2 tablespoons hot sauce
- 1 tablespoon Dijon mustard
- 3 (15-ounce / 425-g) cans sodium-free navy or white beans, drained
- 1 tablespoon chopped fresh oregano

Directions
- Add the oil to a big saucepan and place it over medium-high heat.
- For around three minutes, sauté the onion and garlic until they are transparent.
- Bring to a boil after adding the sweet potatoes, chopped tomatoes, tomato paste, sugar, hot sauce, and mustard.
- For ten minutes, simmer the tomato sauce over low heat.
- After adding the beans, simmer for a further ten minutes.
- Serve after adding the oregano.

Per Serving
calories: 256 | fat: 2.1g | protein: 15.1g | carbs: 48.1g | fiber: 11.9g | sugar: 8.1g | sodium: 150mg

Veggie Fajitas with Guacamole

Prep time: 10 minutes | Cook time: 15 minutes | Serves 4

Ingredients

For the Guacamole:
- 2 small avocados pitted and peeled
- 1 teaspoon freshly squeezed lime juice
- ¼ teaspoon salt
- 9 cherry tomatoes, halved

For the Fajitas:
- 1 red bell pepper
- 1 green bell pepper
- 1 small white onion
- Avocado oil cooking spray
- 1 cup canned low-sodium black beans, drained and rinsed
- ½ teaspoon ground cumin
- ¼ teaspoon chili powder
- ¼ teaspoon garlic powder
- 4 (6-inch) yellow corn tortillas

Directions

How to Prepare Guacamole
- Mash the avocados, lime juice, and salt in a medium basin using a fork.
- Add the cherry tomatoes and stir gently.

To Prepare the Fajitas

- Slice the onion, green bell pepper, and red bell pepper into ½-inch pieces.
- A big skillet should be heated to medium heat. Apply cooking spray to the cooking surface once it's heated. Add the beans, peppers, and onion to the skillet.
- Stir in the garlic powder, chili powder, and cumin.
- Cook, covered, stirring halfway through, for 15 minutes.
- Place guacamole and other desired toppings on top of the tortillas after dividing the fajita mixture evenly among them.

Per Serving
calories: 270 | fat: 15.1g | protein: 8.1g | carbs: 29.9g | fiber: 11.1g | sugar: 5.0g | sodium: 176mg

Spaghetti Squash and Chickpea Bolognese

Prep time: 5 minutes | Cook time: 25 minutes | Serves 4

Ingredients
- 1 (3- to 4-pound / 1.4- to 1.8-kg) spaghetti squash
- ½ teaspoon ground cumin
- 1 cup no-sugar-added spaghetti sauce
- 1 (15-ounce / 425-g) can low-sodium chickpeas, drained and rinsed
- 6 ounces (170 g) extra-firm tofu

Directions
- Set the oven's temperature to 400°F (205°C).
- Halve the squash lengthwise. Remove the seeds with a scoop and throw away.
- Place the squash pieces cut-side down on a baking pan after seasoning them with cumin. For twenty-five minutes, roast.
- In the meantime, add the chickpeas and spaghetti sauce to a medium pot that has been heated over low heat.
- Gently squeeze out any extra water from the tofu after pressing it between two sheets of paper towels.
- After 15 minutes of cooking, crumble the tofu into the sauce.
- Take the squash out of the oven and use a fork to form thin strands through the flesh of each half.
- Place a quarter of the sauce on top of each of the four parts of "spaghetti."

Per Serving

calories: 276 | fat: 7.1g | protein: 14.1g | carbs: 41.9g | fiber: 10.1g | sugar: 7.0g | sodium: 56mg

Chimichurri Dumplings

Prep time: 20 minutes | Cook time: 15 minutes | Serves 8 to 10

Ingredients
- 4 cups water
- 4 cups low-sodium vegetable broth
- 1 cup cassava flour
- 1 cup gluten-free all-purpose flour
- 2 teaspoons baking powder
- 1 teaspoon salt
- 1 cup fat-free milk
- 2 tablespoons bottled chimichurri or sofrito

Directions
- Heat the water and broth in a big pot over medium-high heat until they slowly boil.
- Mix the cassava flour, baking powder, all-purpose flour, and salt in a large bowl.
- Whisk the milk and chimichurri until they are well blended in a small bowl.
- To get a firm dough, gradually stir the wet components into the dry ingredients.
- Pinch off a tiny piece of dough with clean hands. Roll into a ball, then gently press into a disk in the palm of your hand. Continue until there is no more dough.
- One by one, carefully put the dumplings into the boiling liquid. Simmer, covered, until the dumplings are cooked through, about 15 minutes. A fork inserted into the dumpling should come out clean as a test.
- Warm up and serve.

Per Serving
calories: 133 | fat: 1.1g | protein: 4.1g | carbs: 25.9g | fiber: 3.1g | sugar: 2.0g | sodium: 328mg

Redux Okra Callaloo

Prep time: 15 minutes | Cook time: 25 minutes | Serves 6

Ingredients

- 3 cups low-sodium vegetable broth
- 1 (13.5-ounce / 383-g) can light coconut milk
- ¼ cup coconut cream
- 1 tablespoon unsalted non-hydrogenated plant-based butter
- 12 ounces (340 g) okra, cut into 1-inch chunks
- 1 small onion, chopped
- ½ butternut squash, peeled, seeded, and cut into 4-inch chunks
- 1 bunch collard greens, stemmed and chopped
- 1 hot pepper (Scotch bonnet or habanero)

Directions

- Put the vegetable broth, butter, coconut milk, and coconut cream in an electric pressure cooker.
- Arrange the collard greens, squash, okra, onion, and entire hot pepper in layers.
- Set the pressure valve to sealing and close and lock the lid.
- Cook for 20 minutes using the Manual/Pressure Cook setting.
- Release the pressure quickly after the cooking is finished. Gently take off the lid.
- Take out the hot pepper and throw it away. The callaloo should be carefully moved to a blender and blended until smooth. Serve with grits on the side.

Per Serving

calories: 174 | fat: 8.1g | protein: 4.1g | carbs: 24.9g | fiber: 5.1g | sugar: 10.0g | sodium: 126mg

Baby Spinach Mini Quiches

Prep time: 10 minutes | Cook time: 15 minutes | Serves 6

Ingredients

- Nonstick cooking spray
- 2 tablespoons extra-virgin olive oil
- 1 onion, finely chopped
- 2 cups baby spinach
- 2 garlic cloves, minced
- 8 large eggs, beaten
- ¼ cup whole milk
- ½ teaspoon sea salt
- ¼ teaspoon freshly ground black pepper
- 1 cup shredded Swiss cheese

Directions

- Set the oven temperature to 375°F (190°C). Apply nonstick cooking spray to a 6-cup muffin pan.
- Heat the olive oil in a big skillet over medium-high heat until it shimmers. Cook for 4 minutes or until the onion is tender. Add the spinach and simmer for about a minute, stirring, until the spinach is tender. Put the garlic in there. Cook for 30 seconds while stirring continuously. Take off the heat and let it to cool.
- Beat the eggs, milk, salt, and pepper in a medium-sized bowl.
- Incorporate the cheese and chilled veggies into the egg mixture. Fill the muffin pans with the mixture using a spoon. Bake for about 15 minutes, or until the eggs are set. Before serving, let it sit for five minutes.

Per Serving

calories: 220 | fat: 17.1g | protein: 14.1g | carbs: 3.9g | fiber: 1.0g | sugar: 2.9g | sodium: 238mg

Vegetable Egg Bake with Avocado

Prep time: 5 minutes | Cook time: 25 minutes | Serves 4

Ingredients

- 2 tablespoons extra-virgin olive oil
- 1 red onion, chopped
- 1 green bell pepper, seeded and chopped
- 1 sweet potato, cut into ½-inch pieces
- 1 teaspoon chili powder
- ½ teaspoon sea salt
- 4 large eggs
- ½ cup shredded pepper Jack cheese
- 1 avocado, cut into cubes

Directions

- Set the oven's temperature to 350°F (180°C).
- Heat the olive oil in a sizable, ovenproof skillet over medium-high heat until it shimmers. Add the bell pepper, sweet potato, onion, chili powder, and salt. Cook, stirring regularly, for approximately ten minutes, or until the veggies begin to brown.
- Take off the heat. In the pan, arrange the vegetables in four wells. In each well, crack an egg. Around the borders of the eggs and on top of the vegetables, scatter the cheese.
- Bake for about 10 minutes, or until the eggs are set.
- Before serving, place one avocado on top.

Per Serving

calories: 285 | fat: 21.1g | protein: 12.1g | carbs: 15.9g | fiber: 5.1g | sugar: 10.0g | sodium: 265mg

Tofu and Broccoli Stir-Fry

Prep time: 10 minutes | Cook time: 20 minutes | Serves 4

Ingredients

- 3 tablespoons extra-virgin olive oil
- 4 scallions, sliced
- 12 ounces (340 g) firm tofu, cut into ½-inch pieces
- 4 cups broccoli, broken into florets
- 4 garlic cloves, minced
- 1 teaspoon peeled and grated fresh ginger
- ¼ cup vegetable broth
- 2 tablespoons soy sauce (use gluten-free soy sauce if necessary)
- 1 cup cooked brown rice

Directions

- Heat the olive oil in a large skillet over medium-high heat until it shimmers. Stir in the broccoli, tofu, and scallions and simmer for about 6 minutes, or until the veggies start to soften. Stir continually for 30 seconds after adding the ginger and garlic.
- Stir in the rice, soy sauce, and broth. To thoroughly heat the rice, cook it for an additional one to two minutes while stirring.

Per Serving
calories: 235 | fat: 13.1g | protein: 11.1g | carbs: 20.9g | fiber: 4.1g | sugar: 12.3g | sodium: 362mg

Mushroom and Broccoli Frittata

Prep time: 5 minutes | Cook time: 10 minutes | Serves 4

Ingredients
- 2 tablespoons extra-virgin olive oil
- ½ onion, finely chopped
- 1 cup broccoli florets
- 1 cup sliced shiitake mushrooms
- 1 garlic clove, minced
- 8 large eggs, beaten
- ½ teaspoon sea salt
- ½ cup grated Parmesan cheese

Directions
- On high, preheat the oven broiler.
- Heat the olive oil in a medium ovenproof skillet over medium-high heat until it shimmers.
- Add the broccoli, mushrooms, and onion. Cook, stirring regularly, for about five minutes, or until the veggies begin to brown.
- Cook the garlic for 30 seconds while stirring continuously.
- Spread the vegetables evenly across the pan's bottom.
- In a separate bowl, mix together the eggs and salt while the vegetables are cooking. Over the veggies, carefully pour the eggs. Let the eggs settle over the vegetables while cooking without stirring. Pull the edges away from the pan's sides with a spatula as the eggs start to set around the edges. Allow the raw eggs to run into the gaps by tilting the pan. Continue cooking for another one to two minutes, or until the edges are firm. The tops of the eggs will remain runny.
- Put the pan in the broiler after adding the Parmesan. Broil for about three minutes, or until browned and puffed.
- To serve, cut into wedges.

Per Serving
calories: 281 | fat: 21.1g | protein: 19.1g | carbs: 6.9g | fiber: 2.1g | sugar: 4.0g | sodium: 655mg

Zucchini and Pinto Bean Casserole

Prep time: 15 minutes | Cook time: 15 minutes | Serves 4

Ingredients
- 1 (6 to 7-inch) zucchini, trimmed
- Nonstick cooking spray
- 1 (15-ounce / 425-g) can pinto beans or 1½ cups Salt-Free No-Soak Beans,
- rinsed and drained
- 1⅓ cups salsa
- 1⅓ cups shredded Mexican cheese blend

Directions
- Cut the zucchini into rounds. At least 16 slices are required.
- Apply nonstick cooking spray to a 6-inch cake pan.
- Place the beans in a medium bowl and use a fork to mash some of them.
- Place roughly 4 slices of zucchini on the bottom of the pan. Add roughly half a cup of salsa, half a cup of cheddar, and half a cup of beans. Apply pressure. Continue for two more layers. Add the cheese, salsa, and remaining zucchini. (The top layer is devoid of beans.)
- Place a loose piece of foil over the pan.
- Fill the electric pressure cooker with one cup of water.
- Carefully lower the pan into the pot after setting it on the wire rack. The pressure cooker's cover should be closed and secured. Put the valve in the sealed position.
- Cook for 15 minutes under high pressure.
- Press Cancel once the cooking is finished, then let the pressure drop normally.
- Unlock and take off the lid after the pin drops.
- Using the wire rack's handles, carefully take the pan out of the pot. Before slicing the dish into quarters and serving, let it sit for five minutes.

Per Serving
calories: 251 | fat: 12.1g | protein: 16.1g | carbs: 22.9g | fiber: 7.1g | sugar: 4.0g | sodium: 1080mg

Vegetable Enchilada Casserole

Prep time: 15 minutes | Cook time: 15 minutes | Serves 6

Ingredients
- 1 tablespoon extra-virgin olive oil
- ½ onion, chopped
- 3 garlic cloves, minced
- ½ green bell pepper, deseeded and chopped
- ½ red bell pepper, deseeded and chopped
- 2 small zucchinis, chopped
- 1 (10-ounce / 284-g) can low-sodium enchilada sauce
- 1 (15-ounce / 425-g) can low-sodium black beans, drained and rinsed
- 1 teaspoon ground cumin
- ½ cup shredded Cheddar cheese, divided
- 2 (6-inch) corn tortillas, cut into strips
- ¼ teaspoon salt
- ¼ teaspoon freshly ground black pepper
- Chopped fresh cilantro, for garnish
- Plain yogurt, for serving

Directions
- Bring the broiler to a high temperature.
- In a large ovenproof skillet, heat the olive oil until it shimmers.
- Add the bell peppers, zucchini, onion, and garlic. Sauté for 3 to 5 minutes, or until the onion is transparent.
- Whisk together the tortilla strips, black beans, cumin, ¼ cup of cheese, enchilada sauce, salt, and pepper. Sprinkle the remaining ¼ cup of cheese on top.
- Put the skillet under the broiler and cook for 5 to 8 minutes, or until the cheese is melted.
- Serve with the yogurt on top and garnished with the cilantro.

Per Serving
calories: 172 | fat: 7.2g | protein: 8.3g | carbs: 21.2g | fiber: 7.2g | sugar: 3.2g | sodium: 563mg

Tomato, Lentil and Chickpea Curry

Prep time: 10 minutes | Cook time: 25 minutes | Serves 6

Ingredients
- 1 tablespoon extra-virgin olive oil
- 1 sweet onion, chopped
- 1 teaspoon minced garlic
- 1 tablespoon grated fresh ginger
- 2 tablespoons red curry paste
- ½ teaspoon turmeric
- 1 teaspoon ground cumin
- Pinch cayenne pepper
- 2 cups cooked lentils
- 1 (28-ounce / 794-g) can low-sodium diced tomatoes
- 1 (15-ounce / 425-g) can water-packed chickpeas, rinsed and drained
- ¼ cup coconut milk
- 2 tablespoons chopped fresh cilantro

Directions
- In a large saucepan, heat the olive oil over medium-high heat.
- Stirring occasionally, add the onion, garlic, and ginger and cook for approximately three minutes, or until they are soft.
- Add the cayenne pepper, turmeric, cumin, and red curry paste, and cook for an additional minute.
- Bring the curry to a boil after adding the cooked lentils, tomatoes, chickpeas, and coconut milk and stirring to mix.
- After it begins to boil, lower the heat and simmer it for 20 minutes.
- Garnish with the cilantro and serve.

Per Serving
calories: 340 | fat: 8.2g | protein: 18.2g | carbs: 50.2g | fiber: 20.2g | sugar: 9.2g | sodium: 25mg | Cholesterol: 0mg

Cheesy Quinoa Casserole

Prep time: 20 minutes | Cook time: 30 minutes | Serves 4

Ingredients
- 1 teaspoon extra-virgin olive oil
- ½ sweet onion, chopped
- 2 teaspoons minced garlic
- 2 eggs, whisked
- 2 cups cooked quinoa
- 2 cups cherry tomatoes
- ½ cup low-fat ricotta cheese
- Salt and freshly ground black pepper, to taste
- 1 zucchini, cut into thin ribbons
- ⅛ cup toasted pine nuts

Directions
- Set the oven's temperature to 350°F (180°C).
- In a medium skillet, heat the olive oil over medium-high heat.
- The garlic and onion should be softened after 3 minutes of intermittent stirring.
- Take the skillet off of the burner. Stir to incorporate the cooked quinoa, cheese, cherry tomatoes, and whisked eggs.
- Season with salt and pepper. Pour the blend into a baking dish.
- Add the pine nuts and zucchini ribbons on top. The casserole should be heated through after around 25 minutes of baking in a preheated oven.
- Before serving, let it cool for five to ten minutes.

Per Serving
calories: 305 | fat: 9.3g | protein: 17.2g | carbs: 38.2g | fiber: 4.2g | sugar: 5.2g | sodium: 236mg | cholesterol: 122mg

Zoodles with Beet and Walnut Pesto

Prep time: 20 minutes | **Cook time:** 40 minutes | **Serves 2**

Ingredients
- 1 medium red beet, peeled, chopped
- ½ cup walnut pieces, toasted
- ½ cup crumbled goat cheese
- 3 garlic cloves
- 2 tablespoons freshly squeezed lemon juice
- 2 tablespoons plus 2 teaspoons extra-virgin olive oil, divided
- ¼ teaspoon salt
- 4 small zucchini, spiralized

Directions
- Set the oven temperature to 375°F (190°C).
- Make sure to properly seal the aluminum foil after wrapping the red beet in it.
- Roast till soft, 30 to 40 minutes in a preheated oven.
- When the red beet is ready, put it in a food processor. Add the salt, two tablespoons of olive oil, goat cheese, garlic, lemon juice, toasted walnut, and salt. Pulse until smooth. The beet mixture should be transferred to a small basin.
- In a big skillet, warm the final two teaspoons of olive oil over medium heat. Toss the zucchini in the oil after adding it. Cook, stirring frequently, until the zucchini is tender, 2 to 3 minutes.
- After taking the zucchini off of the stove, transfer it to a platter and cover it with the beet mixture. Serve heated after tossing thoroughly.

Per Serving
calories: 424 | fat: 39.3g | protein: 8.1g | carbs: 17.2g | fiber: 6.2g | sugar: 10.1g | sodium: 340mg

Pita Stuffed with Tabbouleh

Prep time: 20 minutes | Cook time: 0 minutes | Serves 4

Ingredients
- 1 cup cooked bulgur wheat
- 1 English cucumber, finely chopped
- 1 yellow bell pepper, deseeded and finely chopped
- 2 cups halved cherry tomatoes
- ½ cup fresh parsley, finely chopped
- 2 scallions, white and green parts, finely chopped
- Juice of 1 lemon
- 2 tablespoons extra-virgin olive oil
- Salt and freshly ground black pepper, to taste
- 4 whole-wheat pitas, cut in half

Directions
- In a large bowl, mix together the bulgur wheat, bell pepper, cucumber, tomatoes, parsley, scallions, lemon juice, and olive oil. To taste, add salt and pepper.
- The pita halves should be placed on a spotless surface. Serve the bulgur mixture right away after dividing it evenly among the pita halves.

Per Serving
calories: 245 | fat: 8.2g | protein: 7.2g | carbs: 39.2g | fiber: 6.2g | sugar: 4.2g | sodium: 166mg

Egg and Pea Salad in Kale Wraps

Prep time: 10 minutes | Cook time: 0 minutes | Serves 2

Ingredients
- 4 hard-boiled large eggs, chopped
- 1 cup fresh peas, shelled
- 2 tablespoons red onion, finely chopped
- ½ teaspoon sea salt
- ¼ teaspoon paprika
- 1 teaspoon Dijon mustard
- 1 tablespoon fresh dill, chopped
- 3 tablespoons mayonnaise
- 2 large kale leaves

Directions
- In a bowl, combine all the ingredients except the kale leaves. Mix thoroughly by stirring.
- After dividing and spooning the mixture onto the kale leaves, wrap the mixture in the leaves by rolling them up. Serve right away.

Per Serving
calories: 296 | fat: 18.2g | protein: 17.2g | carbs: 18.2g | fiber: 4.2g | sugar: 12.3 | sodium: 623mg

Jicama with Guacamole

Prep time: 5 minutes | Cook time: 0 minutes | Serves 4

Ingredients

- 1 avocado, cut into cubes
- Juice of ½ lime
- 2 tablespoons finely chopped red onion
- 2 tablespoons chopped fresh cilantro
- 1 garlic clove, minced
- ¼ teaspoon sea salt
- 1 cup sliced jicama

Directions

- Add the avocado, lime juice, cilantro, garlic, onion, and salt to a small bowl. Use a fork to lightly mash.
- For dipping, serve with the jicama.

Per Serving

calories: 74 | fat: 5.1g | protein: 1.1g | carbs: 7.9g | fiber: 4.9g | sugar: 3.0g | sodium: 80mg

Peppers with Zucchini Dip

Prep time: 10 minutes | Cook time: 0 minutes | Serves 4

Ingredients
- 2 zucchini, chopped
- 3 garlic cloves
- 2 tablespoons extra-virgin olive oil
- 2 tablespoons tahini
- Juice of 1 lemon
- ½ teaspoon sea salt
- 1 red bell pepper, seeded and cut into sticks

Directions
- Put the zucchini, garlic, olive oil, tahini, lemon juice, and salt in a food processor or blender. Blend until it's smooth.
- For dipping, serve with the red bell pepper.

Per Serving

calories: 120 | fat: 11.1g | protein: 2.1g | carbs: 6.9g | fiber: 2.9g | sugar: 4.0g | sodium: 155mg

Simple Parmesan Acorn Squash

Prep time: 10 minutes | Cook time: 20 minutes | Serves 4

Ingredients

- 1 acorn squash (about 1 pound / 454 g)
- 1 tablespoon extra-virgin olive oil
- 1 teaspoon dried sage leaves, crumbled
- ¼ teaspoon freshly grated nutmeg
- ⅛ teaspoon kosher salt
- ⅛ teaspoon freshly ground black pepper
- 2 tablespoons freshly grated Parmesan cheese

Directions

- Remove the seeds from the acorn squash after halves it lengthwise. To make four wedges, cut each half in half. If it's easy, snap off the stem.
- Put the olive oil, salt, pepper, nutmeg, and sage in a small bowl. Apply the olive oil mixture to the squash's sliced sides.
- After adding one cup of water, place a wire rack or trivet inside the electric pressure cooker.
- Arrange the squash skin-side down in a single layer on the trivet.
- The pressure cooker's cover should be closed and secured. Put the valve in the sealed position.
- Cook for 20 minutes under high pressure.
- Press Cancel to immediately release the pressure after the cooking is finished.
- Unlock and take off the lid after the pin drops.
- Remove the squash from the pot with care, then top with the Parmesan and serve.

Per Serving

calories: 86 | fat: 4.1g | protein: 2.1g | carbs: 11.9g | fiber: 2.1g | sugar: 0g | sodium: 283mg

Hearty Corn on the Cob

Prep time: 10 minutes | Cook time: 20 minutes | Serves 12

Ingredients
- 6 ears corn

Directions
- Take out the corn's husks and silk. Each ear should be cut or broken in half.
- Fill the electric pressure cooker's bottom with one cup of water. Put in a trivet or wire rack.
- Put the corn cut-side down and erect on the rack. The pressure cooker's cover should be closed and secured. Put the valve in the sealing position.
- Cook for five minutes under high pressure.
- Press Cancel to immediately release the pressure after the cooking is finished.
- Unlock and take off the lid after the pin drops.
- Take the corn out of the pot using tongs. Serve right away after seasoning to taste.

Per Serving
calories: 64 | fat: 1.1g | protein: 2.1g | carbs: 13.9g | fiber: 0.9g | sugar: 5.0g | sodium: 12mg

Garlicky Broccoli Florets

Prep time: 10 minutes | Cook time: 25 minutes | Serves 8

Ingredients
- 2 large broccoli heads, cut into florets
- 2 tablespoons extra-virgin olive oil
- 3 garlic cloves, minced
- ¼ teaspoon salt
- ¼ teaspoon ground black pepper
- 2 tablespoons freshly squeezed lemon juice

Directions
- Prepare a large baking sheet with parchment paper and preheat the oven to 425°F (220°C).
- Combine the broccoli, garlic, olive oil, salt, and pepper in a big bowl.
- Toss thoroughly until all of the broccoli is coated. Place the broccoli on the baking sheet that has been prepped.
- Broccoli should be browned and forktender after about 25 minutes of roasting in a preheated oven, with a halfway turn.
- Take out of the oven, transfer to a platter, and allow to cool for five minutes. Drizzle with lemon juice and serve.

Per Serving
calories: 33 | fat: 2.1g | protein: 1.2g | carbs: 3.1g | fiber: 1.1g | sugar: 1.1g | sodium: 85mg

Roasted Cauliflower with Lime Juice

Prep time: 5 minutes | Cook time: 25 minutes | Serves 4

Ingredients
- 1 cauliflower head, broken into small florets
- 2 tablespoons extra-virgin olive oil
- ½ teaspoon salt, or more to taste
- ½ teaspoon ground chipotle chili powder
- Juice of 1 lime

Directions
- Prepare a large baking sheet with parchment paper and preheat the oven to 450°F (235°C). Put aside.
- In a large dish, toss the cauliflower florets in the olive oil. Add salt and chipotle chili powder for seasoning.
- On the baking sheet, arrange the cauliflower florets.
- Bake for 15 minutes in a preheated oven, or until just beginning to brown. After about ten minutes, turn the cauliflower over and keep roasting it until it is crisp and soft.
- Take out of the oven and sprinkle with salt if necessary.
- Serve after cooling for six minutes and drizzling with lime juice.

Per Serving
calories: 100 | fat: 7.1g | protein: 3.2g | carbs: 8.1g | fiber: 3.2g | sugar: 3.2g | sodium: 285mg

Vegetable Stuffed Portobello Mushrooms

Prep time: 5 minutes | Cook time: 20 minutes | Serves 4

Ingredients

- 8 large portobello mushrooms
- 3 teaspoons extra-virgin olive oil, divided
- 4 cups fresh spinach
- 1 medium red bell pepper, diced
- ¼ cup feta cheese, crumbled

Directions

- Set the oven temperature to 450°F (235°C).
- Remove the mushroom stems and place them on the cutting board. Using a spoon, remove the gills and dispose of them. Use two teaspoons of olive oil to coat the mushrooms.
- Place the mushrooms on a baking pan, cap side down. Bake for 20 minutes in a preheated oven, or until the top is browned.
- The remaining olive oil should be heated in a skillet over medium heat until it shimmers.
- After adding the red bell pepper and spinach to the skillet, cook for 8 minutes, turning periodically, until the veggies are soft.
- Transfer to a bowl and turn off the heat.
- After taking the mushrooms out of the oven, place them on a platter. Stuff the mushrooms with the veggies using a spoon, then top with the feta cheese. Warm up and serve.

Per Serving
calories: 118 | fat: 6.3g | protein: 7.2g | carbs: 12.2g | fiber: 4.1g | sugar: 6.1g | sodium: 128mg

Sauteed Green Beans with Nutmeg

Prep time: 15 minutes | Cook time: 5 minutes | Serves 4

Ingredients
- 1 tablespoon butter
- 1½ pounds (680 g) green beans, trimmed
- 1 teaspoon ground nutmeg
- Sea salt, to taste

Directions
- In a large skillet over medium heat, melt the butter.
- For five minutes, while turning constantly, sauté the green beans in the melted butter until they are crisp but still soft.
- Add salt and nutmeg and stir to combine.
- Before serving, take off the heat and let it cool for a few minutes.

Per Serving

calories: 83 | fat: 3.2g | protein: 3.2g | carbs: 12.2g | fiber: 6.1g | sugar: 3.2g | sodium: 90mg

Minestrone

Prep time: 10 minutes | Cook time: 20 minutes | Serves 4

Ingredients

- 2 tablespoons extra-virgin olive oil
- 1 chopped onion
- 1 red bell pepper, seeded and chopped
- 2 minced garlic cloves
- 1 (14-ounce / 397-g) can crushed tomatoes
- 2 cups green beans (fresh or frozen; halved if fresh)
- 6 cups low-sodium vegetable broth
- 1 tablespoon Italian seasoning
- ½ cup dried whole-wheat elbow macaroni
- Pinch red pepper flakes (or to taste)
- ½ teaspoon sea salt

Directions

- In a large saucepan, heat the olive oil over medium-high heat until it shimmers.
- The bell pepper and onion should begin to soften after about three minutes of frequent stirring.
- Stirring occasionally, add the garlic and simmer for 30 seconds until fragrant.
- Bring the mixture to a boil after adding the tomatoes, green beans, vegetable broth, and Italian spice.
- Season with salt, red pepper flakes, and elbow macaroni. Continue cooking until the macaroni is cooked through, about 8 minutes, stirring now and again.
- Before serving, take off the heat and transfer to a big bowl to cool for six minutes.

Per Serving

calories: 202 | fat: 7.2g | protein: 5.2g | carbs: 29.2g | fiber: 7.2g | saturated fat: 1g | sodium: 479mg

Veggie and Tofu Stir-Fry

Prep time: 10 minutes | Cook time: 10 minutes | Serves 4

Ingredients

- 3 tablespoons extra-virgin olive oil
- 12 ounces (340 g) firm tofu, cut into ½-inch pieces
- 4 cups broccoli, broken into florets
- 4 scallions, sliced
- 1 teaspoon peeled and grated fresh ginger
- 4 garlic cloves, minced
- 2 tablespoons soy sauce (use gluten-free soy sauce if necessary)
- ¼ cup vegetable broth
- 1 cup cooked brown rice

Directions

- In a large skillet, heat the olive oil over medium-high heat until it simmers.
- Stir-fry the broccoli, tofu, and scallions for six minutes, or until the veggies begin to soften.
- Stir continuously for about 30 seconds after adding the ginger and garlic.
- Add the brown rice, vegetable broth, and soy sauce and fold to combine. Cook for a further one to two minutes, or until the rice is thoroughly heated, after stirring to mix.
- Before serving, allow it to cool for five minutes.

Per Serving
calories: 238 | fat: 13.2g | protein: 11.1g | carbs: 21.2g | fiber: 4.2g | saturated fat: 2g | sodium:360 mg

Vegetable Baked Eggs

Prep time: 5 minutes | Cook time: 25 minutes | Serves 4

Ingredients

- 2 tablespoons extra-virgin olive oil
- 1 red onion, chopped
- 1 sweet potato, cut into ½-inch pieces
- 1 green bell pepper, seeded and chopped
- ½ teaspoon sea salt
- 1 teaspoon chili powder
- 4 large eggs
- ½ cup shredded pepper Jack cheese
- 1 avocado, cut into cubes

Directions

- Set the oven's temperature to 350°F (180°C).
- In a big skillet, heat the olive oil until it shimmers over medium-high heat.
- Add the bell pepper, onion, sweet potato, salt, and chili powder.
- Cook, stirring frequently, until the veggies are gently browned, about 10 minutes.
- Take off the heat. Create four wells in the vegetables with the back of a spoon, then crack an egg into each well. Over the veggies, scatter the crumbled cheese.
- Bake for approximately ten minutes in a preheated oven, or until the eggs are set and the cheese has melted.
- Before serving, take off the heat and top with the avocado.

Per Serving
calories: 286 | fat: 21.3g | protein: 12.3g | carbs: 16.2g | fiber: 5.2g | saturated fat g | sodium: 266mg

Sautéed Collard Greens and Cabbage

Prep time: 10 minutes | Cook time: 10 minutes | Serves 8

Ingredients

- 2 tablespoons extra-virgin olive oil
- 1 collard greens bunch, stemmed and thinly sliced
- ½ small green cabbage, thinly sliced
- 6 garlic cloves, minced
- 1 tablespoon low-sodium soy sauce

Directions

- In a large skillet, heat the olive oil over medium-high heat.
- The collard greens should begin to wilt after about two minutes of sautéing in the oil.
- Add the cabbage and stir to combine. Lower the heat to medium-low, cover, and simmer until the greens are tender, 5 to 7 minutes, stirring occasionally.
- Stir to mix after adding the soy sauce and garlic. Cook until aromatic, approximately 30 seconds more.
- Transfer to a plate and serve after taking off the heat.

Per Serving
calories: 73 | fat: 4.1g | protein: 3.2g | carbs: 5.9g | fiber: 2.9g | sugar: 0g | sodium: 128mg

Roasted Delicata Squash with Thyme

Prep time: 10 minutes | Cook time: 20 minutes | Serves 4

Ingredients

- 1 (1- to 1½-pound) delicata squash, halved, seeded, and cut into ½-inchthick strips
- 1 tablespoon extra-virgin olive oil
- ½ teaspoon dried thyme
- ¼ teaspoon salt
- ¼ teaspoon freshly ground black pepper

Directions

- Set the oven's temperature to 400°F (205°C). Put parchment paper on a baking pan and set it aside.
- In a large bowl, combine the squash strips, salt, pepper, thyme, and olive oil. Toss until the squash strips are completely coated.
- Arrange the squash strips in a single layer on the baking sheet that has been prepared. Roast, turning the strips halfway through, until gently browned, about 20 minutes.
- After taking it out of the oven, serve it on plates.

Per Serving

calories: 78 | fat: 4.2g | protein: 1.1g | carbs: 11.8g | fiber: 2.1g | sugar: 2.9g | sodium: 122mg

Roasted Asparagus and Red Peppers

Prep time: 5 minutes | Cook time: 15 minutes | Serves 4

Ingredients
- 1 pound (454 g) asparagus, woody ends trimmed, cut into 2-inch segments
- 2 red bell peppers, seeded, cut into 1-inch pieces
- 1 small onion, quartered
- 2 tablespoons Italian dressing

Directions
- Set the oven's temperature to 400°F (205°C). Put parchment paper on a baking pan and set it aside.
- In a large bowl, combine the asparagus, peppers, onion, and dressing; toss to combine.
- Place the veggies on the oven sheet and roast them for 15 minutes or so, or until they are tender. Using a spatula, turn the vegetables once while they are cooking.
- Serve after transferring to a sizable platter.

Per Serving
calories: 92 | fat: 4.8g | protein: 2.9g | carbs: 10.7g | fiber: 4.0g | sugar: 5.7g | sodium: 31mg

Tarragon Spring Peas

Prep time: 10 minutes | Cook time: 12 minutes | Serves 6 (½ cup each)

Ingredients

- 1 tablespoon unsalted butter
- ½ Vidalia onion, thinly sliced
- 1 cup low-sodium vegetable broth
- 3 cups fresh shelled peas
- 1 tablespoon minced fresh tarragon

Directions

- In a skillet over medium heat, melt the butter.
- For approximately three minutes, or until transparent, sauté the onion in the heated butter, stirring now and then.
- Whisk thoroughly after adding the veggie broth. Stir the tarragon and peas together in the skillet.
- Cover, lower the heat to low, and continue cooking until the peas are soft, about 8 more minutes.
- Serve the peas warm after letting them cool for five minutes.

Per Serving
calories: 82 | fat: 2.1g | protein: 4.2g | carbs: 12.0g | fiber: 3.8g | sugar: 4.9g | sodium: 48mg

Week 1 Shopping List

- Mixed berries
- Ground flaxseed
- Unsweetened coconut flakes
- Unsweetened plain coconut milk
- Leafy greens (kale, spinach)
- Unsweetened vanilla nonfat yogurt
- Ice
- Rolled oats
- Walnut pieces
- Pepitas
- Salt
- Ground cinnamon
- Ground ginger
- Coconut oil
- Unsweetened applesauce
- Vanilla extract
- Dried cherries
- Whole-wheat pastry flour
- Almond flour
- Granulated sweetener
- Baking powder
- Fresh lemon zest
- Baking soda
- Ground nutmeg
- Eggs
- Skim milk
- Plain Greek yogurt
- Fresh blueberries
- Chia seeds
- Clementine
- Kiwi
- Coconut cream
- Sweet onion
- Red bell pepper
- Feta cheese
- Parsley
- Black pepper
- Red onion
- Green bell pepper
- Cheddar cheese
- Canned black beans
- Enchilada sauce
- Corn tortillas
- Cilantro

Week 1 Meal Plan

Days	Breakfast	Lunch	Snack	Dinner
Day 1	Coconut and Berry Smoothie	Spanakopita Frittata	Blueberry Muffins	Herbed Beans and Brown Rice Bowl
Day 2	Walnut and Oat Granola	Crispy Pita with Canadian Bacon	Apple and Bran Muffins	Enchilada Black Bean Casserole
Day 3	Greek Yogurt and Oat Pancakes	Eggplant and Bulgur Pilaf	Coconut and Chia Pudding	Tomato, Lentil and Chickpea Curry
Day 4	Apple and Pumpkin Waffles	Zoodles with Beet and Walnut Pesto	Jicama with Guacamole	Ratatouille Egg Bake
Day 5	Cottage Pancakes	Linguine with Kale Pesto	Peppers with Zucchini Dip	Vegetable Enchilada Casserole
Day 6	Buckwheat Crêpes	Tofu and Broccoli Stir-Fry	Baby Spinach Mini Quiches	Vegetable Baked Eggs
Day 7	Tropical Yogurt Kiwi Bowl	Zucchini and Pinto Bean Casserole	Garlicky Broccoli Florets	Quinoa and Lush Vegetable Bowl

Week 2 Shopping List

- Chia seeds
- Liquid stevia
- Clementine
- Kiwi
- Coconut cream
- Sweet onion
- Red bell pepper
- Garlic
- Black pepper
- Feta cheese
- Parsley
- Sun-dried tomatoes
- Almonds
- Dry whole-wheat linguine
- Whole-wheat flour
- Greek yogurt
- Oats
- Apples
- Vanilla extract
- Baking powder
- Baking soda
- Eggs
- Skim milk
- Ground cinnamon
- Ground nutmeg
- Canned lentils
- Diced tomatoes
- Chickpeas
- Red curry paste
- Turmeric
- Ground cumin
- Cayenne pepper
- Zoodles (zucchini noodles)
- Fresh basil
- Baby spinach
- Bell peppers
- Parmesan cheese
- Coconut oil
- Cottage cheese
- Lemon

Week 2 Meal Plan

Days	Breakfast	Lunch	Snack	Dinner
Day 1	Coconut and Chia Pudding	Eggplant and Bulgur Pilaf	Fresh Apple Slices with Almond Butter	Ratatouille Egg Bake
Day 2	Greek Yogurt and Oat Pancakes	Linguine with Kale Pesto	Mixed Nuts and Dried Berries	Tomato, Lentil and Chickpea Curry
Day 3	Tropical Smoothie Bowl	Spinach and Feta Stuffed Peppers	Chia Seed Pudding with Clementine Slices	Lemon Herb Quinoa Salad with Chickpeas
Day 4	Apple Cinnamon Overnight Oats	Sun-Dried Tomato and Spinach Wrap	Hummus with Carrot Sticks	Coconut Curry Lentil Stew
Day 5	Banana Almond Butter Toast	Zoodles with Lemon Basil Pesto	Greek Yogurt with Honey and Walnuts	Stuffed Bell Peppers with Lentils and Spinach
Day 6	Spinach and Feta Omelette	Roasted Veggie and Quinoa Bowl	Avocado and Tomato on Whole Grain Crackers	Spicy Chickpea Stir-Fry
Day 7	Cottage Cheese with Fresh Berries and Almonds	Zucchini and Feta Frittata	Lemon Basil Roasted Almonds	Cauliflower and Sweet Potato Curry

Week 3 Shopping List

- Pecans
- Fresh mint leaves
- Egg whites
- Spinach
- Dijon mustard
- Baby spinach
- Swiss cheese
- Red onion
- Yellow zucchini
- Eggplant
- Zucchini
- Oregano
- Basil
- Red pepper flakes
- Red lentils
- Tomato paste
- Coconut milk
- Almond flour
- Baking powder
- Ground cinnamon
- Vanilla extract
- Greek yogurt
- Apples
- Cottage cheese
- Avocado
- Bell peppers
- Brown rice
- Portobello mushrooms
- Broccoli
- Soy sauce
- Sesame oil
- Tofu
- Fresh ginger
- Vegetable broth
- Pine nuts
- Shredded Parmesan cheese
- Green beans
- Scallions

Week 3 Meal Plan

Days	Breakfast	Lunch	Snack	Dinner
Day 1	Apple Cinnamon Pancakes	Spinach and Swiss Cheese Quiche	Greek Yogurt with Chopped Pecans	Eggplant and Red Lentil Stew
Day 2	Avocado Toast with Cherry Tomatoes	Zucchini Noodles with Pesto and Cherry Tomatoes	Cucumber Slices with Hummus	Tofu Stir-Fry with Broccoli and Brown Rice
Day 3	Tropical Smoothie Bowl with Fresh Mint	Grilled Portobello Mushroom Burger	Almond Flour Muffins	Red Lentil Coconut Curry
Day 4	Spinach and Feta Omelette	Quinoa Salad with Avocado and Pine Nuts	Sliced Apple with Almond Butter	Roasted Veggie Stuffed Peppers
Day 5	Cottage Cheese with Fresh Blueberries and Almonds	Roasted Veggie and Brown Rice Bowl	Lemon Basil Roasted Almonds	Zoodles with Tomato Basil Sauce
Day 6	Banana Walnut Pancakes	Lentil Salad with Feta and Mint	Broccoli Florets with Greek Yogurt Dip	Spinach and Red Lentil Stew
Day 7	Scrambled Egg Whites with Spinach and Feta	Eggplant and Zucchini Lasagna	Sliced Bell Peppers with Tahini Dip	Mushroom and Pine Nut Risotto

Week 4 Shopping List

- Tomatoes
- Pepper Jack cheese
- Avocado
- Tofu
- Broccoli
- Scallions
- Fresh ginger
- Soy sauce
- Vegetable broth
- Brown rice
- Green bell pepper
- Sweet potato
- Shredded Parmesan cheese
- Portobello mushrooms
- Cucumber
- Kalamata olives
- Pine nuts
- Quinoa
- Lemon
- Red bell pepper
- Tahini
- Zucchini
- Baby spinach
- Chickpeas
- Garlic
- Basil
- Red onions
- Coconut oil
- Black beans
- Tortilla wraps
- Mango
- Cilantro
- Lime
- Oats
- Cinnamon
- Maple syrup

Week 4 Meal Plan

Days	Breakfast	Lunch	Snack	Dinner
Day 1	Spinach and Avocado Smoothie	Quinoa Salad with Chickpeas and Red Bell Pepper	Cucumber Slices with Tahini Dip	Stuffed Portobello Mushrooms with Parmesan and Spinach
Day 2	Oatmeal with Cinnamon and Fresh Mango	Brown Rice and Black Bean Burrito Wraps	Roasted Chickpeas with Paprika	Broccoli and Tofu Stir-Fry with Soy-Ginger Sauce
Day 3	Avocado Toast with Red Onion and Basil	Lemon Herb Quinoa with Roasted Vegetables	Carrot Sticks with Hummus	Zucchini Noodles with Tomato Basil Sauce and Pine Nuts
Day 4	Chia Seed Pudding with Mango and Lime Zest	Spinach and Tomato Frittata	Mixed Nuts and Dried Fruit	Sweet Potato and Chickpea Curry
Day 5	Banana Maple Oatmeal	Greek Salad with Cucumber, Tomato, and Kalamata Olives	Roasted Sweet Potato Slices with Avocado	Roasted Cauliflower Steaks with Lemon Tahini Dressing
Day 6	Berry Smoothie Bowl with Granola	Tofu and Spinach Wrap with Red Bell Pepper	Apple Slices with Almond Butter and Cinnamon	Chickpea and Spinach Stir-Fry with Brown Rice
Day 7	Scrambled Tofu with Spinach and Tomato	Zucchini and Avocado Salad with Lemon Dressing	Sliced Bell Peppers with Black Bean Dip	Grilled Portobello Mushrooms with Basil Pesto and Quinoa

Video Bonus!!!

 10 Life-Changing Glucose Hacks: easy tricks that will change how you feel forever

 Glucose Goddess: The Alarming New Truth About Grapes! These 10 Hacks To Strip Fat Without Exercise!

 Sugar CRAVINGS: 3 reasons you have them and the proven science to destroy them

 You CAN Beat Diabetes & Insulin Resistance: Simple Hacks to Reverse It NOW!

Thank You

As I bring this book to completion, I am filled with immense gratitude for the support and inspiration that made this project possible.

First and foremost, a heartfelt thank you to Jessie Inchauspe. Your groundbreaking work and dedication to spreading the message of balanced glucose levels have inspired countless individuals, including myself, to prioritize health and wellness in a realistic and sustainable way. This cookbook is a testament to your influence, and I am grateful for the path you have paved in nutritional science.

To my readers, thank you for choosing to embark on this journey with me. Your curiosity, commitment to health, and willingness to explore new habits motivate me every day. I hope these recipes not only nourish your body but bring joy and simplicity to your daily life.

A special thank you to my family and friends who supported me throughout the writing and testing phases of this cookbook. Your feedback, patience, and unwavering belief in me gave this project the energy it needed to come to life.

To my editor and publishing team, thank you for your meticulous attention to detail, creativity, and guidance. Your collaboration turned these ideas into a polished work I'm proud to share.

Lastly, I extend my deepest gratitude to all the experts, farmers, and food producers who work tirelessly to provide fresh, wholesome ingredients. Your passion fuels not only our kitchens but the health and well-being of communities worldwide.

May this cookbook serve as a source of inspiration, helping you make choices that align with your wellness journey. Here's to balanced living, one recipe at a time.

With all my gratitude,

Michelle C. Huff.

Printed in Great Britain
by Amazon

56793073R00051